The Forked Path: The Journey of Dark Miss

Melissa Munro

BookLeaf Publishing

India | USA | UK

The Forked Path: The Journey of Dark Miss
© 2024 Melissa Munro

All rights reserved.

Melissa Munro asserts the moral right to be identified as author of this work.

Presentation by *BookLeaf Publishing*

Web: www.bookleafpub.com

E-mail: info@bookleafpub.com

ISBN: 9789363304437

First edition 2024

To my loving partner: Without you, I would not have had the happy ending I enjoy everyday. To my beloved pack: thank you for catching me when I fall.

ACKNOWLEDGEMENT

To every other survivor standing tall today despite their past, I see you and your strength is what true beauty is made of. Photography credit for my headshot goes to Willow H. Thank you helping see my own beauty through the power of your lens.

PREFACE

These are the words of a survivor. The Forked Path will give you a front row seat to the Journey of Dark Miss. From a broken little girl to a Caretaking Dominatrix, let us adventure together!

An Acolyte Born

So very young to be broken
What an Old Soul they'd say
Despised as I refused to be their clay
Wild magic poured from a budding seersD eyes
An unknown Goddess answers the little ones
cries

An eternal mother for the forsaken daughter was
net
Spirits gave love and a new path was set
The old ways gained a warrior with a high level
debt
Knees bent for magic and earth, never bells and
church
An acololyte born from a loved starved search.

Dirty Snow

2

Lying there I didn't realize I had a choice
I thought I trusted his hands, I knew his face
A lifetime of ignorance to hide behind
Was all he needed to ignore my voice
The dirty snow forever stained upon my mind
For my sacred virginity i mourned and pined
Discarded on winters forest floor
Jagged scars shattered across my souls core
Innocence lost, no longer a girl I'm now
redefined
A date rape survivor

My Own Heroine

Swagger, Romance, Charm and Sex
The mask of a love bombing narcissist
Painstakingly crafted by a sadists mind
Expertly sculpted to dazzle one blind
My pride shredded when he brought another in
Fists and knives perverted my flesh
His other sin

Wounded prey a target for a rapid predator
Still he failed to kill me and I opened fates door
His sad life forfeit, his choice, his misfortune
May I beacon survivors to hope by the light
Of the Storm Moon
I get to live in a world where he didn't win
Standing tall as my own heroine

Deaths Misery

Fingers dig at her arms
Clutching for dear life
A tear streaked face
Devoid of hope

She wanted to give in
Just let the world go
But something kept her here
Despite valiant efforts otherwise

In the depths of my heart I know
I survivor for more than myself
Even still, I chose to live for me
I choose life over deaths misery

Game Over

I am so sick of being your fucking martyr
This is not a trade, negotiation or barter
There is no pain, remorse or sorry
I did what I did and I go no farther

I am free of all that harms
And have always been immune to your charms
I should have known that this couldn't be
But alas I thought, of course...wait and see

He almost left me because of you
But there you were without a clue
You didn't know what it did to me
Because I refused to set you free

I tried to leave without a fight
It didn't work, it wasn't right
I wanted to walk away with light
Not done within the cover of night

I stand for me and mine
Your spot is at the back of the line
I will not bend, break or bow
I hope your happy its over now

So go move your pieces on your board
I refuse to play and we cannot afford
To sacrifice all to just save the one
Its over, I'm beyond being done

Greedy Devil

The sadistic vampire
Dipping into my energy
Drinking and bleeding
Until my husk was dusty
Ready to crumble
At the slightest breeze

He took, I gave, until my table was bare
The river of my heart ran cool
He wore the mask of Pan
'Twas just a greedy devil in disguise
Desperate enough to believe his own lies

The Next Step

A brand new path to forge
Born of the ash, lays in front of me
The opportunity to leave behind toxicity

Glancing back, over my shoulder and all I can
see
The clash of discourse and strife devoid of
tranquility
My patient heart finally out grew
I trudge onward, my journey anew

With each step I have clarity and can better
know my own voice
A dappled forest lush with possiblility
Where I'll cut a new trail
Leading forward to living authentically
Nature sings in triumph while my soul vibrates
Embracing my choice

Earthsong

Bring your spirit back to honor and earth
Reflect with remorse to know growth
Hold in mind the depth of her worth

The musky scent of leaves in fall
Snowcapped mountains of winter standing tall
The first of springs crocus, shooting free
A harvest of summers bounty of plenty

Let Earthsong ring clear as a bell
Feel her heartbeat
The nurturing call
The enduring spell
Sink into the grass
Rest your back to a tree
Give appreciation to the north
Where earths power does dwell

Winds of Change

Bring your spirit back to truth with air
Take a moment to breathe deeply with
purposeful care
Welcome the winds of change to blow steadily
through
Gusting and carrying away all that doesn't serve
you
By feathered friend prayers can be carried
anywhere
Keep the words you speak compassionate,
loving and true
Create your world of justice based in balance to
be fair

War Fire

Bring to your spirit a fiery transition
Watch as the hungry flames lick wood
Best to be open to spiritual vision
With the heat and inferno withstood
Provoke creativity and kindle the spark
Marvel at the light as it beats back the dark
By souths gate you'll find the passion
As you invoke the power of transmutation
Fire burns away malice and the battle is won

Healing Seas

12

Bring to your spirit the cleansing of the seas
Let the salty waves wash away pain
Encouraging to bring about ease
River or lake, waterfall or bay
Let the waters heal you of yesterday
From the west gate mercy breaks free
Dance under refreshing showers of rain
Reverently listen to the waves
Give your soul the peace it craves

Children of the Goddess

Sacred holy mother of mine
I honor the Goddess, the oldest of the divine
Joyful maiden, patient mother and ancient crone
The awakened listen deep to their ancestors call
Honor the seasons as the tapestry of life is so
colorfully sown
and She who bears too many names to invoke
them all
We see her power winter and spring, summer
and fall

I am a child, practitioner of the ways of old
Blessed to witness many mysteries untold
The stardust of Magick holds me enthrall
By spell and herb, by will and rite my soul is is
consoled
When spirit guides your hand, heart and life
You'll know less pain, less anger and strife
Blessed be the children of the goddess
Let us join hands and proudly stand tall

From Hell Come Dreams

Flashing strobing lights
Glittering off pasties fishnets and tights
Music pounds against your ears
But music pounding is not all you'll hear
As you wander towards the dungeon here

Flashy swirling strobe lights
Reflect off pasties and fishnet tights
Music echos and the bass pounds
Listen closely for more interesting sounds
Whimpering submissives moan as the whips
crack
They would squirm and scream
And they always came back
A cold mistress guided the night
Her stare made bottoms tremble in fright
Her work was pure artistry to behold
I knew right then how I wanted my path to
unfold

No longer hidden in the bedroom ever so shy
But here in front of the crowd on Club Hells
Stage
Giving pain and pleasure to make patrons fly
That first Mistress inspired my entire life

She showed me a path other than a humble wife

None filled her boots perfectly
Even I couldn't stay permanently
But when heartbreak shook me body and mind
Where did I go? What did I find?
The legacy night was alive and well
Though no longer housed at the infamous club
Hell
Come to KiNK at Alchemy where the proud
freaks dwell

We've made a home and a loving family
Giving kinksters a safe place to be
Partners in paddles now own this night
Where our fantasies unfold and our dreams take
flight

Dear One

16

My battered soldier of Old Leather
True Subject on blended on knee
Their devotion inspires me
A muse for an artist
Their body my canvas
Their word our bond
My collar sits against the throat
That speaks with reverence

My Prision

Lost in the tower, my conjured trick
I made it stone to mortar, will to brick
Thoughts to spell, may the power rise
Moment by moment the darkness flies

Thorned rose, deadly nightshade enterwine
Up rocks to the terrace they climb
My single portal to world below
The front door baracade long ago

My chains hold me fast and tight
I cast them of impenetrable night
I refuse to struggle, squirm and twist
Held so closed, as clenching fist

Safely enclosed, encircled by bitten chill
Comfortably entrapped within my skill
Here it the quiet, the tranquil
Leaving it would be futile

The cliff below would slice me to shards
And climbing down posioned vines is not in the
cards
The door barred from both exit and entry
While I feel complete, I'm unable to flee

Have You Met Consent?

One touch does not mean two
Listen closely with the utmost care
To what others actually gift you
Your body is Yours alone to share

Consent is the two way street
Where every lover and play partner
On equal terms must meet
Without coercion or clever lure

A hug is not permission to kiss
A kiss is not an invitation of more
How is this a lesson people miss
A violation
can send a body and mind to war
And it's a bitter cold comfort
To be a survivor

Mating

The subtle caress of teasing lips
Descend upon my needy clit
Sensuous, fluttering pressure
Feather soft fairy wings
Kissing against my needy skin
A hand snakes my throat
His firm mouth and teasing tongue
Steal the scream of a moan
Right from my throat.
My body erupts
Tremors of pleasure quake
Coursing through me
Every touch sends me deeper
Part of my spirit dives under
Taken by the riptide
The rest of me floats until flying.
Every thrust brings me higher.
 Into the nights shadows my soul soars
The never ending orgasm steals me
 Long after mating is done

Captive Play

Fear pricks sharp holes in my mind
As the icy steel caresses me
Pressing, poking and scratching
The trust it takes, the power of will
To enjoy this ride while perfectly still
That level of intrinsic skill so hard to find

While the blade is steady in his hand
So is my life glittering bright
Reflected, glinting off the clubs strobe light
My sweat slicked skin
Flushed from punishment
Blushing and shuddering
So close I could cry

My body never truly content
A rushing pulse creeps into my throat
His hands become a cherished necklace
My aching limbs twitch
Where am I
Face crushed in his chest
His heart races with mine
Our never ending experiment

Come Dance

Bruising fingertips
Stamp the flesh
Marks of conquer
Decorate the skin

Overstimulated cries
Echoing in the music
Seeping into the dungeon walls
The anthem of pain laced pleasure

Desperate squirms
Of bottoms pushed
Riding the edge
Guided over by practiced hands

Tranquil warm waves
Floating up, lifting higher
Unbound from the mundane
Energy soars to dance with the stars

Welcome Tributes

Hands over head
Bound by leather and chain
I welcome tributes
to my dungeons domain
Almost gentle hands
learn your bodies tales
Long before you'll feel
The fall of my flails

Start out with sensation
An easy caress
The introductory massage
Given to assess
Where best to land the blows
And offer the gift of pain
Slide into space with me
Before you name
Our time together
As a painful blessing
Or a healing bane

Freed

My panting breath
echoes upon stone walls
No screams pass my lips
My eyes are dry
Until I hear the hunters calls

A gasp breaks the silence
Challenged while chained
This is not fair, not right
I yearn to hide, to run
To take my comfort in the night

The magic awakens
I feel the pulse, I know the beat
I throw off my shackles
Hot tears stream my cheeks
Unused and untried my legs buckle

Eyes widen as the call breaks again
The tower shakes in anticipation
Impatient with my spell
No longer tolerant of my pain
The stones quake, the walls crumble

I can barely walk through flying debris
And now I'm forced to tumble

To dart, to scream, to fall
My sanctuary had been my hell
The pain had been my lock

My body plummets with the stone
Wind whistling hauntingly around me
Pebbles and shards cut my skin
The vines tangle against my chains
I squeeze my eyes shut against the horror

My heart beat passes the time
Each breath taken is tainted with blood
I retch and vomit and pass the poison
Unable to believe my mind
Unwilling to believe my ears

I awaken

The stones have become a path
A garden so lush, so filled of spring
Roses entwined with wrought iron
My shackles needed somewhere to go
Herbs flower, a crow calls, dawn breaks

A breath of life is taken
The battle of self is won
Time to dream new dreams
Trembling and humble I stand
Freed